FINANCIAL TIMES

Management Briefings

The Justification and Costing of Information Systems

CHRIS CHALCRAFT

FT
PITMAN
PUBLISHING

London • Hong Kong • Johannesburg • Melbourne • Singapore • Washington DC

PITMAN PUBLISHING
128 Long Acre, London WC2E 9AN
Tel: +44 (0)171 447 2000
Fax: +44 (0)171 240 5771

A Division of Pearson Professional Limited

First published in Great Britain 1997

ISBN 0 273 63216 7

British Library Cataloguing in Publication Data
A CIP catalogue record for this book can be obtained from the British Library.

10 9 8 7 6 5 4 3 2 1

Printed and bound in Great Britain

The Publishers' policy is to use paper manufactured from sustainable forests.

bs

The Justification and Costing of Information Systems

Financial Times Management Briefings are happy to receive proposals from individuals who have expertise in the field of management education.

If you would like to discuss your ideas further, please contact Andrew Mould, Commissioning Editor.

Tel: 0171 447 2210
Fax: 0171 240 5771
e-mail: andrew.mould@pitmanpub.co.uk

Contents

About the author

Chris Chalcraft is currently employed as the Information Systems manager at Collmain PLC. He holds a history degree and is a qualified Certified Accountant. His career started in accountancy with MFI at their head office in London. He then gradually migrated away from accountancy into information systems over a number of years. For the past three years, he has been Project Manager responsible for downsizing bespoke legacy systems onto standard packages. This also involved establishing a company-wide data warehousing application.

Readers of this report can contact the author at the following addresses:

Business:
Collmain PLC
Dubarry House
Newtown Road
Hove
BN3 7AY

Telephone: (01273) 221448
Fax: (01273) 207059

Home:
58 Fort Road
Newhaven
East Sussex
BN9 9EJ

Telephone: (01273) 512016

1   Introduction

This briefing report covers four main areas of information systems (IS) expenditure:

1   The requirement to prepare a business case for expenditure

2   Areas of justification to consider for making the spend

3   Potential costs involved

4   How information systems (IS) expenditure is reported in financial statements

This is followed by thirteen appendices, which illustrate various items discussed throughout this briefing report.

The Business Case

The business case for IS expenditure is discussed in Chapter 2, focusing on the question 'What is a business case?' It also discusses what the business case should contain, to gain approval for IS expenditure.

Areas of Justification for IS Expenditure

Chapters 3 to 8 focus on certain areas of justification and discuss how monetary values may be applied to them. Everything in business has to be paid for. Therefore, you need to present a business case justifying, in financial terms, why you want to spend money. This business case should also state what you want to spend the organisation's money on.

The actual items involved in IS expenditure are generally similar: new hardware or new software. However, the justification will vary. Sometimes, the reason for requesting new hardware is not because the old hardware does not function; rather, the old hardware costs too much to maintain. In other instances, hardware upgrades will be requested because the existing hardware is incapable of running newer software.

In the first instance, cost is the driver; in the second, performance is the driver. The first instance is easier to evaluate. What is the cost of the new hardware? The second instance is broader, because it involves new hardware to run new software.

This briefing report focuses on six main areas of justifying IS expenditure. The chapters are arranged in a specific order, to reflect the ease with which costs and benefits may be calculated. The discussion is wide ranging and explores six main areas to consider when preparing a case to justify investment in IS.

The discussion opens in Chapter 3 with business efficiencies in general; the next two chapters look at IS expenditure in particular. Chapter 6 considers the benefits of management information and data warehousing. Chapter 7 looks at the impact on employees within the organisation, and Chapter 8 looks at benefits that may occur in the future through investment today.

Chapter 3 – Improve Business Administration

This chapter covers general business issues. How may the investment in IS improve business processes? In particular, this briefing report discusses how business overheads may be reduced in general. The costs and benefits involved in any justification should be straightforward to calculate.

Chapter 4 – Save Money on Information Systems (IS)

This chapter considers how the investment in IS may be recouped in part by reducing running costs. Many large organisations set a target of reducing operating systems expenditure by a fixed amount each year. If the target is, say, a 10% reduction each year then it is unlikely that this will be achievable without fresh investment. The costs and benefits here should be relatively easy to calculate.

Chapter 5 – Provide Secure Core Systems

This chapter reviews the benefits to an organisation of possessing secure information systems. The benefits in this area only become apparent when things go wrong.

Chapter 6 – Improve Management Information

This chapter discusses the benefits to the business of having better and quicker management information. The provision of better information to managers should mean that they demand more and more information. This information should provide the business with a better competitive edge in the market place. To place a specific value on this benefit is not easy. In the worst case though, without it, an organisation may go out of business. To provide this information, it may be worth building a data warehouse. The data stored may then be analysed by the business managers using their preferred package.

Chapter 7 – Intangible Benefits

This chapter is concerned with how the investment will benefit members of the organisation, i.e. how their morale and efficiency may be improved.

Chapter 8 – Gateway to the Future

This chapter considers the benefits that may occur in the future. In particular, future upgrades and enhancements should be easier and cheaper.

When you prepare your business case, one or more of the areas listed above should be covered. Normally, the more of those items listed, the greater the spend and the more complex the implementation will be.

When considering the justification, it is worth thinking about building a **costs and benefit matrix**, which will assist you in determining where to direct your organisation's finite cash and time resources. This matrix should help you to identify which items of expenditure will best improve business performance.

A mythical project involving 50 users is used to illustrate the topics discussed in this briefing paper. This approach is used to illustrate how to justify the investment, and how to cost the expenditure involved in networking these 50 staff.

Potential Costs Involved in IS Expenditure

This section covers two chapters: 9 and 10. Chapter 9 discusses costs which are relatively straightforward to predict. The items involved are hardware, business software, office software and network installation and software. These are described as **certain costs** because they are dependent upon quantity. How many PCs do you plan to buy? How many software licences will you need?

Chapter 10 discusses the other costs involved in IS expenditure: such as initial evaluation, the use of consultants, bespoke software and testing the new systems. These items are described as **uncertain costs** because they are harder to predict as accurately as certain costs. These uncertain costs need to be allowed for; they focus on the costs of implementing IS effectively and without them, the implementation may well fail to deliver the promised benefits.

How IS Expenditure is Reported in Financial Statements

This section covers three chapters: 11, 12 and 13.

Chapter 11 looks at the capital investment appraisal of IS expenditure. It is a discussion and illustration of how the total costs and benefits of IS expenditure may be appraised. The purpose is to establish whether the business gains or loses in monetary terms from the expenditure.

Chapter 12 covers how companies report on IS expenditure in their annual published accounts. It explains how to decide what elements of expenditure must be charged to the business's profits for the year in which the expenditure occurs. It also illustrates how the capital element of the expenditure may be spread over a number of years.

Chapter 13 discusses how the Inland Revenue treats expenditure on IS. It compares the treatment adopted by the Inland Revenue to that allowed under accountancy rules.

Conclusion

The overall investment in IS should be presented as a positive action, and not simply as another inevitable burden on the profits of the organisation. For it to be viewed in this positive light, user's expectations of what the software may deliver – and when – must be realistic. The benefits promised in the justification *must* be delivered. If this happens, then future investment is more likely to be forthcoming.

2 Making the business case

Introduction

A business case should be put together before any significant time or money is spent on IS. This discipline of justifying expenditure should be applied to *all* areas of business. Often though, it is in the area of IS expenditure that the most rigorous justification occurs. This is not unreasonable; IS investment is not cheap. In the past, decision makers were not always aware of all the potential costs. They have grown more cautious and cynical about the wonders of IT, and this cynicism has been fuelled by their not gaining all of the benefits promised in the past.

In the light of this, it is now customary for all significant IS expenditure to expect executive approval. Most organisations now expect a cost and benefit analysis for any major IS investment. What is significant will depend on the size of the organisation. In my organisation, the definition of what is significant is 'any projects that will take longer than one man day to complete'. I cost information work at £50 per hour, which approximates to the current market rate for employing outside contractors to do the work.

To obtain executive approval for IS expenditure, a business case must be prepared. This business case is then reviewed. The purpose behind preparing the business case is to enable the executive – the decision makers – within the organisation to make an informed decision as to the costs and benefits of the proposed expenditure. This decision will sometimes be 'yes'; sometimes it is 'no'. If a case is agreed, the work will be prioritised, and scheduled into the IS development timetable.

The business case is prepared by the user department requesting the work, but the IS department assists in preparing costings and in suggesting alternatives. The responsibility for preparing the justification though, rests with the user department. They must justify why they need the work done, and the business case must state the benefits of doing the work. It must also state clearly the consequences to the business of *not* doing the work.

If a business case states both the benefits and the consequences of not agreeing the recommendation, the decision makers are informed of the potential gains *and* potential costs of the proposal. The executive must be made aware of the consequences of their decision; when a recommendation is turned down they must understand the business risk. By being informed, they should be better prepared to accept this business risk.

Where the answer is 'yes' then the benefits, the justification, must be realistic and achievable within the budget agreed. It is most important to have this agreed at the outset. Without this, **scope drift** is likely to occur. This means that the IS department and the user have totally different perceptions of what the end product should be. When this happens, user acceptance testing may well be very prolonged. Indeed the IS investment may be totally wasted if the end user department does not use the systems provided.

Items to Include in the Business Case

The business case should answer these questions:

- What is the justification behind the spend?

- Are there any alternatives to what is being proposed?

- What are the consequences of doing nothing?

- Which other departments or business functions may be affected?

- What are the benefits of the expenditure?

- What is the cost of the expenditure?

What is the Justification Behind the Spend?

This section of the business case should explain clearly the business need to be addressed.

For example, you may be requesting a telesales system to keep track of the conversion of enquiries to sales orders. Currently, you may be using a spreadsheet to record details of telesales enquiries. Current volumes may be manageable using a spreadsheet, but now, with the prospect of increased volumes you may think that a properly designed database is needed to handle the volumes more efficiently.

The specific business areas involved should be covered, and the proposal should state why the work is needed. For example, current volumes may mean the department is spending too much time collating information rather than pursuing business leads.

The justification should include what the work is meant to achieve, and state for what area of the business. Often the justification will be based on internal business needs; for example, the existing information systems may be unable to cope with the current needs of the business. Sometimes the justification may be outside the control of the business; it may arise from the marketplace. For example, your competitors may start to offer a particular service to their customers; to remain competitive your organisation now needs to do the same. Another external source forcing change may be government legislation; you may be compelled to record and report certain information.

To summarise, there are three main areas that drive business change in information systems:

- Internal business pressures

- Pressure from competitors

- Government legislation

Are there any Alternatives to what is being Proposed?

Your proposal should state your preferred solution. However, there will normally be alternatives to what you propose, and you must consider these other solutions to the problem.

For example, if the volumes of work have increased then simply increasing staff numbers may solve the problem without having to change the computer system. An alternative solution may involve a change in a business process.

What are the Consequences of Doing Nothing?

This section of the business case should focus on the costs of doing nothing. What will be the consequences to the business if your proposal is turned down? How could the business suffer if no action is taken? Is it likely that the opportunity to make significant savings will be lost? Will the business suffer if the proposal is rejected? Would the consequences be terminal to the future of the business?

You should concentrate on specifics. State clearly, if this is the case, that the customer base will be eroded because the organisation is no longer competitive.

You should also discuss just how urgent you need this business change. Consider whether the proposal could be deferred for six months without any adverse consequences. This should provide evidence to the executives as to the urgency of the business need. Is it really vital for this work to be carried out now? Or, is it the case that while it is not needed immediately, it will be in the medium term?

By stating clearly – and unemotionally – the consequences of doing nothing, or deferring the proposal, the executives are made aware of the potential costs of their decision. The executives' time is valuable; therefore, it makes sense to give them the complete picture. This information will also assist in deciding how soon the work must be done after the request is approved. It also helps to provide a measure of how much the business should invest in any solution.

Which Other Departments or Business Functions may be Affected?

Often IS expenditure in one area will affect other areas of the business, and those areas should be listed. It may be that the climate is not right for them to experience any change at the present time. The biggest brake on IS investment is the speed at which the organisation is able to absorb change. The business must still continue to function effectively while these changes are implemented. Therefore, careful consideration must be given to the business as a whole.

It may be that these other areas could also gain from the expenditure, so this could add additional weight to your justification.

What are the Benefits of the Expenditure?

This section of the business plan should state specifics; it is not sufficient to make a blanket statement such as: 'We will make more money.' The proposal should estimate the potential revenue increase, say, for the telesales database. The business plan should state clearly how this expenditure should enable more leads to be turned into orders. Similarly, you should state the potential value of leads currently being lost to the organisation. If the investment is made, how many new orders do you expect to result that are currently being lost to the business?

If the proposal is aimed at improving business efficiencies then the business plan should state the future cost savings anticipated. How much money in salaries will be saved? By how much will overtime be reduced? What proportion of administration costs could be switched towards customer-facing activities?

It is important to identify which areas of the organisation will gain. For example, you should illustrate how much money will be saved if duplication within the organisation is reduced. Where you propose to save on head count then this is relatively straightforward to calculate. Estimates should include what staff numbers will be after the implementation. Other items will be more judgmental and subjective.

- How do you value the savings made through quicker and simpler information systems?

- How do you value improved staff morale?

- These items, though difficult to estimate with any accuracy, *do* need to have a value put against them. Then the benefits of the investment may be measured at a later date.

What is the Cost of the Expenditure?

The costs involved in implementing a business case for IS will vary depending upon the scope of the request. The scope may be very broad, possibly involving a review of the organisation's IT strategy. It may be very narrow, e.g. requiring a new report to pay commission to sales staff on a new basis.

Calculating the cost of hardware needed is relatively straightforward. The cost of PCs is easily established by asking suppliers to tender for a certain specification and quantity, e.g. 50 486 PCs each with 8MB of RAM and 500MB hard discs. Similarly, the actual cost of standard software packages is easy to obtain.

What is much harder to cost is exactly what is involved in successfully implementing hardware or software. To cost accurately, time and thought needs to be invested in the early stages; otherwise, costs not budgeted for will appear at a later stage. If insufficient money is available for these items then not all of the benefits outlined in the business case will be realised. If sufficient money is found and invested, then the costs may exceed those originally forecast and approved.

It is probably at this stage of preparing the business plan that the user will need assistance from the IS department to identify areas of expenditure that may otherwise be overlooked.

Where possible, it helps to translate the work involved into man (woman) hours. I then apply an across-the-board charge of £50 for each man (woman) hour for preliminary costings, which approximates to the current market rate. This procedure will enable a financial budget to be prepared to support the business case.

3   Improving business administration

Introduction

This chapter discusses those areas of business improvement that may be used to justify expenditure. Any justification for the expenditure should be measured against the improvements to the processes within the business.

- Does the business benefit in a positive way from the expenditure?

- Does it make more money and, consequently, more profit?

This benefit may arise from making more sales and increasing turnover. It may occur because you need fewer staff to administer the business and can reduce costs.

In the past, for many organisations, software has been seen as an opportunity to streamline staffing. Management identified routine and repetitive tasks, and then purchased, or had written, software that performed these tasks more quickly and efficiently than existing staff. Examples would include payroll or payment of suppliers. This type of software could be termed **basic business operating software**; the tasks it was designed to perform were of an operational nature.

Those days, when those simple repetitive tasks were easy to identify, have now gone. Today, most companies will be on their second or third generation software systems. Often though, the systems installed are either function or department based. The IS installed does not encompass all of the company's activities, and often they do not embrace the greater part of the organisation.

In the past, companies have installed, for example, separate systems for sales, stock control and finance. These systems existed independently of each other and little thought was given to transferring data between them electronically.

Today, organisations are investing in new software as a means of integrating the separate distinct department-based software applications installed in the past. It is in this integration of the old, separate and function-based systems that the business processes may be improved by investment in new IS.

Organisations are also looking for software to perform both operational and strategic functions: operational functions enable the business to run smoothly on a day-to-day basis; strategic functions need software to analyse how the business is actually performing.

The challenge facing organisations today, therefore, is to select and implement software that satisfies *both* operational and strategic needs. The core operational software must perform routine tasks quicker and more effectively; it must also be capable of storing all transaction data. At the same time, the historical information produced by the operational systems must be capable of being summarised and analysed. This information should form the basis from which business decisions are made.

The current buzz words include executive information systems (EIS), drill down, etc. However, the first requirement for *any* of these systems is the capture of base transaction data.

The selection process for new software is not easy. You could buy one single, all encompassing, product, say R/3 supplied by SAP – if your organisation has a large amount of money and time to invest. However, medium and even larger organisations can obtain the same functionality, at significantly less cost. This cost will not be inconsequential, and therefore you must justify your proposal to spend the profits of your organisation.

This chapter now looks at four areas where internal business processes may be considerably improved by investment in new IS:

1   Improving business processes and efficiency

2   Business process re-engineering

3   Creation of an organisation-wide database

4   Enabling management to focus on its core business

Improving Business Processes and Efficiency

Having an organisation with different computer databases for different parts of the business is a recipe for

- duplication

- inconsistency

- avoidance of responsibility and

- lack of control.

Duplication will arise because the same item of data will have to be entered separately into each system wherever it is needed. For example, a customer's details may be entered in three separate systems: sales, stock control and finance. On a more profound level, the Sales Department may have performance figures which differ significantly from those held by the Finance Department. The Sales Department may see a healthy order level; the Finance Department may see a series of unprofitable sales.

Where separate databases exist then the need will arise to transfer some data from one system to another. Often, this transfer is done manually by re-inputting some of the data. The manual transfer of data between systems may well cause log jams in the paperwork chain. The processing of a new order may be delayed until the details are manually transferred from one system to another, and this may have a detrimental effect on customer service. Often, items 'disappear' unnoticed at this stage – unnoticed, that is, until an irate customer telephones.

The more duplication of data entry then the greater the overhead on staff time. The only reason you need these staff is to redo work that someone else within the organisation has already done. Also, the more complex the organisation, then the greater the controls necessary to ensure that data is transferred correctly from one system to another.

Inconsistency will occur if each of these departments has a different idea of precisely what customer information is important to them, since this normally determines what data they input. The quality of the information will also vary; there may be misspellings or incorrect address details, and so the overall data quality will vary from system to system. Often, the quality of the data input is dependent on the input clerk or junior manager. The coding structure used to set up this information, and the key fields by which any data consolidation will rise or fall, may also be inconsistent between systems.

Avoidance of responsibility happens because data ownership within the organisation is unclear. Who is responsible for ensuring that a customer's address details are correct? Sales or Invoicing? Who is responsible for ensuring that all orders are invoiced? No one person owns *all* the various aspects of data within an organisation. Managers will often assume that another manager is responsible. The importance of data quality may only become apparent when the need to look at historical data in a new light arises. Then everyone stands around, shaking their heads and saying: 'If only we had done it that way in the first place.'

Lack of control will arise if one part of the organisation mistakenly assumes that another department is responsible for a particular process. What may actually happen is that this process *only* occurs intermittently, when someone remembers to do it.

New technology may also remove the need for Head Office to be involved until orders are received. Field sales staff using laptops and portable printers may now deliver quotes on site, direct to the customer. This offers two direct benefits to the business: it speeds up the delivery of price information to the customer; and removes the need to assign staff at Head Office to type the quotes.

The use of modern technology appropriate to the business may thus enable businesses to steal a competitive advantage over their competitors. A quicker turn around may be an important selling point in a competitive market.

To summarise, improving business processes and efficiency includes:

- speeding up the flow of information around the company

- removing layers of administration

- using laptops and portable printers to deliver quotes quicker

- reducing 'log jams' in the paperwork chain

- relieving existing systems which may be under pressure

- reducing duplication of effort and data inconsistencies.

Business Process Re-engineering

Business process re-engineering means ensuring that an organisation has two basic qualities: simplicity and effectiveness. This is not a new concept; however, achieving these two basic qualities is not easy.

Organisational structures tend to evolve and grow from two main causes: business pressures and flexible managers. Thus processes within an organisation tend to be bent and distorted to accommodate these pressures. The organisational structure and process can then lose its coherence – its internal logic. Often, this lack of coherence is not recognised. The job gets done. The company makes a profit, and the additional overhead cost is ignored until profits decline and something *has* to be done.

One of the greatest benefits of introducing new software systems is that the organisation is forced to look afresh at all business processes. However, companies make plans, draw flow charts and draft new organisational structures. These are all discussed, amended and then ... inertia. The nettle is not grasped. Personality, preference and dislike of the unknown come into play. The risks involved in re-engineering are deemed greater than the hoped-for benefits.

However, if organisations are to benefit fully from the introduction of new IS then a reform of those business processes affected is essential. A review of the business processes necessary for an organisation to function effectively and efficiently need not be a Herculean task; neither need it cost a huge amount.

What *is* needed is support and recognition from the executive that a review is needed. Today, to gain ISO9000 certification, all business processes should be recorded. It is fast becoming necessary to hold an ISO9000 certificate before work can be gained from major customers. You may use this process of review to combine the two. Have you seen how much it may cost to achieve ISO9000? It is not cheap! So why not gain something useful, internally, from the process as well?

The benefits of business process engineering are as follows:

•   Major systems change should also involve looking at the structure of the company.

•   It is an ideal opportunity to combine the two.

•   It is a good time to question whether a process actually benefits the business.

Creation of an Organisation-wide Integrated Database

As discussed earlier, organisations aiming to improve business processes and efficiency are currently looking at removing duplicated effort and data inconsistencies. These will often result from a company having several separate computer databases for different areas of the business. Examples are sales, marketing, manufacturing, personnel, stock control and finance. Each major business area will have its own computer systems. This spread of disparate systems will have evolved as each major business area has purchased, or designed and had built, a system that suits their specific operating and reporting needs.

This will obviously create duplicated data entry and storage. Examples include a salesperson's details. Some of this information could appear on sales, marketing and personnel systems. A product may appear in manufacturing, stock control and finance. Often this information will involve data of a different quantity and value, in each of the two parallel systems.

This duplication of data may also result in inconsistencies. These will not become apparent until you try to collate information across these separate systems. The sales system may be built around the salesperson's name. The marketing system may use their initials. The personnel system will use the employee number.

It is not difficult to imagine the immediate problems confronting the IS department when asked to provide a report on information relating to sales performance. The report needs to contain details on sales turnover, marketing effort, salary and commission earned by individual salespersons.

Thus, when an organisation has such disparate systems, it will be difficult and expensive to collate information from these separate systems. The lack of consistency in how key information is coded may also mean that management is presented with conflicting, incomplete or incoherent information on which to make business decisions.

To summarise, the benefits of the creation of an organisation-wide database are:

- a single database for all aspects of business

- a single common point of data entry

- speeded up input to system

- reduced duplication of effort

- the removal of inconsistencies.

Enabling Management to Focus on its Core Business

It is also worth considering how much time the organisation devotes to consideration of IS issues. How much of the executives' hours are spent considering changes and improvements to the existing IS? How much time, and therefore money, is spent on reviewing proposals to customise existing in-house IS?

These changes may be necessary to enable the business to compete, but, are the costs of maintaining existing systems diverting resources away from other more fundamentally important aspects of the business?

What is the benefit to the organisation of having an in-house IS development department? Does the organisation actually benefit from operating this unit itself? Would it gain more by handing part of this function over to a specialist firm?

The current trend towards out-sourcing has reached new heights with the recent facilities management (FM) deal between Sears and Arthur Anderson Consulting for £344 million. One of the reasons mooted is the fact that the existing in-house systems were unable to cope with complex stock allocation across the wide range of retail outlets operated by Sears. It may be that, rather than tackle the problem in-house, Sears have chosen to hand responsibility for solving this business problem to a third party.

Organisations are now recognising that their core business is supplying their customers with the products that the company sells. They are now questioning the role of large internal IS departments. For example, consider this question: Does your organisation employ a car mechanic to service your company car?

The benefits of enabling management to focus on its core business are:

- reduction in time spent on designing systems to assist in operating business

- reduction in time taken to enhance systems

- money is spent on increasing market share rather than developing systems.

How to Measure the Benefits of Improving Business Administration

This will depend on how efficiently your business is currently administered. If your organisation is already super-efficient, it may be difficult to identify further savings.

One point to consider is the ratio of support staff to those that generate income. In a simple sales organisation, this may be easy to measure. Organisations engaged in manufacturing or providing services may find this harder to quantify.

You should, however, be aware of industry norms for your market place. If not, then you may be able to obtain some benchmarking figures from the Central Statistical Office.

Improving Business Processes and Efficiency

Consider first the benefit of speeding up the flow of processes through the organisation. Try to establish if the organisation's cash flow could be improved by ensuring that invoices are sent to customers sooner. What would be the value to the business of receiving payments, say, two weeks sooner?

How much would the organisation save in staff costs by removing a layer of administration? How many staff would then be needed? Your business case should state what the reduction in head count will be, and these figures should be costed and included in the justification for the expenditure.

Appendix J gives a table of potential cost savings and assumes that a saving of 3–5% on administration costs is feasible.

Business Process Re-engineering

A change in systems may also be an opportunity to review business processes. You could put a value on this by saying that it should reduce administration costs by a fixed percentage. Most organisations could benefit from an infrequent review of how they function internally. The example in Appendix J suggests a figure of 5–10%.

The business case justification should state precisely how the improvements will reduce staff numbers, so prepare forecast figures of where savings ought to occur. This information will also enable the executive to measure the success of the investment after the implementation has been completed.

A recent example of business process re-engineering is the DSS computerisation of benefit payments. Original estimates in the late 1980s indicated that 20,000 jobs would be saved. Latest figures released indicate that staff numbers have *increased* by 2,000 to 88,000. Not unnaturally, doubts have been expressed about the soundness of the implementation. The costs have also exceeded budget by £750 million pounds.

Creation of an Organisation-wide Integrated Database

The main benefits here are the elimination of duplicated effort and improvements in the quality of core operational data.

To assess the staff savings, it should be possible to identify areas of the business where duplication currently occurs. Having decided which area will do the job in future, you will then not need the resource in the other area(s). This saving should be shown in a cost savings table. Often the duplication will only be part of someone's job; an estimate is therefore needed of what proportion of their job will no longer exist.

The cost savings table in Appendix J assumes an overall saving in administration costs of 2–4%.

Enabling Management to Focus on its Main Business

This is an important area to consider. The management team of a business are an expensive group; their time is valuable. Therefore, information systems that clearly support the business and do not need their constant detailed monitoring are essential. Then the management may focus more thought on customers' needs rather than internal issues.

4   Saving money on information systems (IS)

Many businesses have long recognised IS spending as a significant business cost. Often, the older the system then the dearer the cost of maintaining or enhancing the existing software. This chapter looks at justifying investment in IS to save money in the longer term. This needs to be costed carefully to ensure that the anticipated benefits are both realistic and achievable. However, there a number of cogent arguments that may be put forward to justify the investment.

In particular, four areas are worth considering:

1   Lowering the cost of IS support

2   Lessening reliance on specialist knowledge

3   Out-sourcing or out-tasking

4   Minimising staffing on IS payroll

You should start to notice an overlap as you read through this briefing report. This is because the benefits that occur in one area of justification spill over into other areas. Thus, by improving one part of the IS, you will gain benefits in other areas.

The greater the number of independent IS within the organisation then the greater the costs to support them. This spread of disparate systems within an organisation will also cause a disproportional increase in support costs.

By having fewer types of both hardware and software within a company, obvious financial benefits will follow. There should be material cost savings as you will not need to retain, in-house, such a broad skills base to support the organisation's IS.

Lowering the Cost of IS Support

One obvious benefit of migrating to fewer and more modern operating platforms will be a reduction in the costs of supporting the systems. Modern systems tend to need fewer internal staff to support them on a day-to-day basis.

The day-to-day costs of supporting a legacy system, though, may not be inconsequential. These legacy systems are an organisation's computer systems that have been developed over time. Often they have been customised and tailored to suit the existing business processes very closely. There will probably have been a considerable investment in time and money to create these systems. Often, you will be reliant on a few internal staff or external software houses. The knowledge base may also diminish over time, and the written documentation relating to these systems may be sketchy. A legacy system could be a source of vulnerability for your organisation.

On the matter of hardware, significant performance may be now be obtained from networked PCs supported by file servers. These machines, once installed, should need minimal routine maintenance. In the event of a total crash, RAID (redundant array of inexpensive discs) technology means that the system may be rebuilt rapidly. The support costs for these machines are much less than the cost of supporting proprietary minicomputers.

Similarly, the costs of software support may be significantly reduced by migrating towards standard software packages. The support costs are normally charged annually, based on a percentage, say 20%, of the original purchase price. The cost of this support is therefore fixed, irrespective of how often you contact the software house for help.

The downside is that you lose some control. You are dependent upon the time-scales set by the software house which is working to fix your problem. The costs of this loss of control need to be weighed against the potential benefits.

To summarise then:

- moving to client/server systems reduces hardware maintenance costs;

- software support can be handled by a third party;

- legacy systems are expensive to maintain;

- legacy systems may be expensive to modify or enhance.

Lessening Reliance on Specialist Knowledge

Currently, your organisation may be reliant on certain specialist knowledge. This may have arisen through a lack of documentation when the bespoke systems were developed or subsequently enhanced. The software may be written in older languages and so you maybe rely on a handful of individuals who still understand the code. The software programs themselves may be difficult to follow and expensive to modify. The information provided by the system may no longer be relevant to the needs of the business.

By moving to a more modern software platform, the new systems should come with full documentation. This means that it should be easier to understand both the capabilities and limitations of the new software. The documentation provided may not appear at first glance totally comprehensible! However, as experience and familiarity is gained with the new systems then the knowledge and understanding will increase.

This should enable some of the knowledge to be assimilated by end users, and should cut down time spent by IS answering routine queries. It should also reduce the reliance on pockets of expertise, currently contained within in-house staff or outside third-party suppliers.

Introducing new systems should broaden the base of support available, and so provide a wider pool of expert knowledge. This may give you the flexibility to decide how you want to support your new systems. You should, if you wish, have the flexibility to offer out to tender any future new developments. In short, you may be able to achieve more for less.

Over time, the bespoke development of idiosyncratic and customised systems results in systems unique to a particular organisation. The implementation of new systems should at least provide an opportunity to simplify these systems.

To summarise then:

- the lack of in-house documentation may mean that existing software suppliers are able to charge premium rates for support;

- new systems allow a move away from any over-reliance on software houses.

Out-sourcing or Out-tasking

The implementation of standard software may offer the opportunity to out-source part, or all, of the systems support function. The more standard the package then the easier it should be to out-source. The packages themselves should come with telephone support as standard, which should reduce overall support costs and may remove the need to have an expert on your payroll and on your site.

The term **'out-sourcing'** means transferring responsibility for some or all of the support and development of your IS to a third party. The advantage of this is that the organisation does not have to retain these skills in-house; the disadvantage is a loss of direct control. There may also be cost savings to be gained by the organisation, and these should be included in the business case justifying the expenditure.

In real cash terms, the savings may not be significant. However, what you are able to do is to transfer the systems support headaches to a third party – one whose income is dependent upon providing stable professional systems support. You may therefore obtain a better quality of service externally than internally.

Out-sourcing should provide you with more stable and secure systems. There are now many firms who offer facilities management (FM), and the more standard your software then the cheaper this support should be. FM can remove the need to retain surplus IT staff to cover for holidays, sickness or unexpected additional work.

Some companies are now looking at **out-tasking** – a halfway point between retaining all skills within the business and transferring them all externally. The term out-tasking means transferring to others a selective part of the IS support function, that is, contracting out to a third party those skills that you either do not have in-house or no longer wish to retain internally. This may be because you need this support infrequently. However, because of the critical nature of the function you prefer to retain access to this particular expertise.

The staff that you retain should be those with the most knowledge or use to the business, and will normally be in the area of software applications rather than hardware. They should also act as the liaison between the third party support and the organisation. Out-tasking means that the organisation retains its best skills but transfers those it only needs intermittently.

To summarise then:

- the more standard the platform, the easier it is to out-source support;

- out-sourcing allows an organisation to transfer the headaches of supporting systems to a third party;

- in-house specialist knowledge can be used to refine systems to suit the business;

- IS staff can put their knowledge and experience to best use;

- specific tasks that are too expensive to retain in-house staff for can be out-sourced;

- out-tasking enables an organisation to retain the support at which it is best suited and of most use to the business.

Minimising Staffing on IS Payroll

Payroll is normally the biggest administration cost for any organisation. One common justification for moving to new IS is to reduce the number of in-house IS staff. Using a more standard package, the organisation should need fewer internal quality IS staff and this could provide significant savings.

New IS should reduce the number of support staff on the payroll – staff who do not directly generate income. The required level of expertise should fall through the use of standardised systems, and so it should be possible for the business to recruit lower calibre, and therefore cheaper, staff.

When specific IS projects arise they may be put out to tender, and so additional costs need only be borne when developments are needed.

To summarise then:

- by out-sourcing or out-tasking, heads are removed from payroll;

- organisations only have to pay for specific approved projects;

- you can reduce the number of quality IS staff;

- less skilled staff are needed.

How Much Will the Costs of Maintaining IS be Reduced?

It should be possible to produce fairly accurate estimates of how much the savings should be for each of the three areas of maintaining your IS in the future.

Lowering the Cost of Support

The future costs of systems support should be stated and compared with those currently paid. The past costs of maintaining your systems should be available to you, so compare these historic costs with what you estimate it will cost to support the new systems. A simple table should be sufficient to illustrate these.

The table of potential cost savings in Appendix J assumes a cost reduction of 15–25% per annum.

Lessening Reliance on Specialist Knowledge

The amount saved by being less reliant on specialist knowledge will depend on how much of the existing systems are replaced by standard packages. The greater the change, then the greater the savings should be. Again, a forecast should be prepared, and any assumptions made should be clearly stated.

Savings of 20–30% per annum are assumed in Appendix J.

Out-sourcing or Out-tasking

If your organisation is considering out-sourcing, quotes should be obtained for handing over support to a third party. These quotes can then be compared with the current costs of support.

You should ensure that the level of support offered by an outside source is sufficient for your business needs. The level necessary should be specified in the service level agreement between the users and the IS Department.

It is unlikely that through out-sourcing you will be able to remove *all* IS staff, so, some internal costs will remain. However, these staff may act as the link between the organisation and the out-sourcing company.

If you elect for out-tasking then you will shed some staff but should retain those of most benefit to the business.

Minimising Staffing on IS Payroll

Just how few staff will be needed after the investment in cheaper systems support will depend upon how far-reaching the changes are. Also, if you decide to recruit lower quality staff then an allowance should be made in your costings for recruitment costs.

When considering cost savings, you should include the company's National Insurance (NI) costs and pension costs as well as the salary of staff being made redundant. If appropriate, you should also include savings on the provision of company cars and other benefits enjoyed by senior IS staff.

For employees with more than two years' service, redundancy payments should be included in the costings. You may also decide to make *ex gratia* payments to some staff, these payments being non-taxable to the recipient.

Staff cost savings of 10–20% per annum have been assumed in Appendix J.

5 Providing secure core systems

Introduction

In today's business environment, it is essential for organisations to use computer systems. They are necessary to record all types of transactions – customers, suppliers, employees, products, services, leads, quotes and the list grows longer every day as more tasks are put on to computer. This chapter focuses on justifying expenditure on the basis of providing stable and secure information systems for the organisation.

When you telephone a company to make an enquiry, what is your reaction when the person on the other end of the telephone line says: 'Can you call back later? Our systems are down.'? How impressed are you when they say: 'Can you hold on? I'm just calling up your details now ...' and then, after what seems like several minutes, the clerk at the other end speaks to you again? What image does that convey? Certainly, it does not inspire confidence.

How much time has your organisation lost through staff waiting for the systems to return? What is the cost of, say, ten employees not being able to work for, say, two hours? At £10 per hour per person, £200 is lost! This is without considering the potential revenue that has been lost during that time.

One of the major justifications for installing new systems of both software and hardware is to provide a stable systems platform, one that supports most areas of the organisation. IS have become the hub through which most transactions pass. Organisations need this hub to be transparent and efficient; it should support the business process, not hinder it.

Because systems are now an integral part of most companies, it is becoming commonplace for an agreed level of service and performance to be drawn up between users and the IS department. Indeed, many IS departments within the UK now operate a **service level agreement** with their users. This agreement states clearly what level of IS support the business needs, to function effectively. However, this agreement is only practical and workable if significant investment is made in new systems.

For example, suppose the business demands that the maximum downtime for any function is one hour. This may mean, that to meet this requirement, all the major file servers have to have a backup, or that ten spare PCs are kept in storage, for use in case of a breakdown. This is a business, not an IS, decision.

The existing software may be functional. However, it may not be robust enough to guarantee 95% reliability. If the business demands that software be available for 95% of the time then a more robust software solution will have to be installed. Alternatively, the business must accept that the agreed performance level may be lower, e.g. 75%. Fundamentally, the issue is whether the business loses more through upgrading than it gains through greater reliability. This decision will vary from organisation to organisation.

Less Downtime

The installation of new hardware should mean that the time lost through machine failure – downtime – is minimal. If time is critical then you may choose methods such as disc mirroring whereby all new data is written away to a separate machine. However, for small and medium-sized organisations operating in a non time critical environment this may not be necessary. Modern hardware is very robust, providing, of course, that the machine purchased is sufficient for the task.

This type of networked hardware is not expensive. A powerful network server may be purchased for a few thousand pounds. This should have a useful life of, say, four years and works out at a cost of tens of pounds per day – an insignificant amount when contrasted with the cost of staff sitting idly around.

To summarise then:

- less time is lost through system crashes;

- you can reduce time lost through system maintenance;

- it is quicker and easier to restore from backup tapes or discs.

Fewer Data Losses

Installing a network with centralised backups means security can immediately be improved. Every local PC user can write information to a central file server, and you no longer need to be dependent upon individuals remembering to backup their own work onto floppy discs.

We have all experienced vital word-processed documents or spreadsheets being inadvertently deleted. These may be recovered quickly and simply from the overnight security backup tape. You may have lost that day's work but at least you do not have to start from scratch again.

The main benefit of fewer data losses:

- less time is spent re-keying information.

Improved Data Security

Modern hardware may be purchased with backup streamer tape drives installed. These DAT (digital audio tapes) tapes can hold a huge amount of data. For small or medium-sized companies, entire systems may be backed up on just one or two of these tapes. They cost about £5 each and may be re-used up to at least twenty times – a cost of only 25p to backup large amounts of data.

This means that for a modest sum you are able to backup your system regularly. For an initial outlay of £100 in tapes, you could backup your system every night for a month. How much time did you last waste hunting for files or recreating files accidentally lost? You are also able to archive information from your systems cheaply. The more disc space used then the slower the hardware. Performance begins to degrade after about 70% capacity. If you regularly remove dead transactions to archive, you achieve two things: a fast processor for the users, and a secure archive file.

With the availability of lower cost hard discs, you are also able to reduce the time involved in running backups. It is possible for you to copy all your data from one disc to another, and then transfer this to backup tape later. This means that you can backup your systems regularly during the day. When backups are run, all users should be logged out, but it is possible to do a data backup for one gigabyte, disc to disc, in less than ten minutes, so this should be the maximum time that users need to be logged out. This offers a lower cost solution than disc mirroring or purchasing a second machine, but has to be approved by the business. Is this amount of scheduled downtime acceptable? Is the business prepared to accept the business risk inherent in *not* having a standby machine always available?

Many organisations will have an embryonic disaster recovery plan: 'So we go out and purchase new PCs and load the data on from backup.' Do you understand clearly what computer functions are critical? Are you aware of how what is critical will change during a month? To have a *feasible* disaster recovery plan, you must be able to distinguish clearly between what is essential and what would be nice.

For example, at the beginning of the month, your most critical business activity may be collecting money from customers. At the end of the month, it might be paying suppliers. When would you like this disaster to strike you: pay day or three days before, when the money for the payroll must be transmitted through BACS?

The control of who has access to your systems is easier on modern software platforms. Regular password changes can be enforced. Also, users may be granted access only to those parts of the system that they need. This should minimise any damage that a malicious person may wish to wreak on your systems.

Remote access will also need to be tightly controlled to prevent unauthorised access. There are a number of packages that will handle this. Some of them work by calling back the telephone number dialling in; if the number is not recognised then no connection will be made. (The most effective method I have found is to switch off the modem!)

Computer **viruses** hit the news every so often. The odds on suffering a serious infection are not known but we all know the damage a business could suffer if a virus entered the IS. It is possible to purchase virus checkers that sweep all systems connected to the network; this happens automatically when discs are inserted into the A: drive. These discs are checked for viruses; similarly, any application that has not been checked is verified before it may be used. This software is inexpensive and monthly or quarterly updates come as standard.

So, to summarise, you can improve data security by

- taking efficient and regular backups;

- using CD-ROMs to hold archived information for later analysis;

- creating a realistic disaster recovery plan – at least understanding how your systems work and identifying what really is mission critical;

- restricting access to authorised users;

- using cheap and reliable virus checking software.

Traffic Monitoring

The installation of a local area network (LAN) enables you to monitor the computer systems performance. You can locate bottlenecks and police your systems, without the need for a sophisticated backup team. The basic network software comes with reasonable monitoring capability built in.

For additional performance, there are a number of products available which allow you to record the main indicators of your network's performance and to measure accurately just what activity there is on the system:

- packet rates around the network;

- peaks and troughs of activity;

- when the traffic on the network reaches or exceeds the systems' capabilities.

This monitoring software will also show what programs are most frequently used, and those which are infrequently accessed. This should assist in assessing whether new hardware is needed to improve systems performance, or whether the root cause of a problem is something else, such as intense activity at certain times of the day. A rescheduling of access time slots may alleviate the systems' poor performance problem without any upgrades being purchased.

Similarly, when new developments to the systems are mooted, you will be in a position to review past activity. This should help you to form an opinion as to the merits of the request.

This software will also enable you to takeover a remote PC for fault diagnostics, which could have significant savings in staff time. In effect, it could save staff meandering around the building to a far flung location to fix a fault. Obviously, you cannot handle all problems remotely; users need to see a human being at times, if only to moan at them! You will still need mobile trouble-shooting staff, but you may find though that you need fewer of them.

This software also enables you to monitor the activity on remote PCs, and what software is installed on the local hard disc of a networked PC; this should ensure that only company authorised software is installed on your systems.

What is the Value of Having Secure Core Information Systems?

When all the existing systems are functioning and working correctly, it is difficult to raise this as a benefit. The value of secure and stable systems is only apparent when things have gone wrong. The purpose of this chapter has been to illustrate the benefits of investing in newer technology from the standpoint of security.

Without secure systems the whole organisation could collapse. The values you put into your justification for having secure systems will depend upon the current risk profile of your organisation.

Less Downtime

If your organisation has suffered information systems disruption in the recent past then try to establish how much it cost your organisation. You should try to value sales lost, and add this to the cost of staff sitting around idle. Then, add the cost of catching up when the systems returned. There is also the cost of morale suffering through systems disruption to consider.

These figures should be included in the justification as examples of what it may cost the business if the investment is not approved.

Administration savings of 3–5% per annum have been assumed in Appendix J.

Fewer Data Losses

If there are fewer data losses, there will be less time lost through re-inputting data. Also processes are not delayed until you have caught up with the transactions.

Improved Data Security

It is important to restrict authorised access through the issue of unique passwords. The storing off-site of regular backups of your entire systems provides an insurance policy in event of disaster.

Traffic Monitoring

It may be possible to avoid expensive hardware upgrades by rescheduling work, to alleviate current bottle-necks.

6   Improving management information

So far this briefing report has concentrated on how investment in IS may help to reduce the costs of the organisation. In this area it is easy to reduce costs: you can out-source or out-task your support; you may close down in-house development; you may reduce the number of systems that you need to support.

It is much harder to invest wisely in IS. When considering investment, the requirements of the business must be paramount. There are so many products that appear to be able to assist. It is not easy to identify those that will deliver the greatest benefit for the investment made.

As discussed earlier, the replacement of older systems with newer, more effective, ones is relatively easy – easy, that is, compared to harnessing IT to give your organisation a competitive edge in the marketplace. The purpose of this chapter is to discuss where the investment in IS may be used to drive the business forward.

Large organisations are investing heavily in systems that provide timely information about trading performance. To be successful in business you need two things: customers and products. How you deliver your products to your customer will depend upon the nature of your business. IS, used imaginatively, can provide information about what your customers want and buy. This information can then be fed back into the business process so that more products are sold.

The introduction of new software should enable transactions to be entered more quickly. The validation can ensure that the quality of the information is improved.

Information about an organisation's performance has long been recognised as an essential requirement for managing it effectively. Until recently, the most significant measures were finance based. The discipline of management accounting arose out of the need to strip away the more esoteric accounting conventions. The aim was to see if the company was making money in real terms. Are you generating more cash than you are spending? This chapter discusses how investment in IS may be justified by improving the quality of information provided to the business executive and operational managers.

With the growth in competition, many organisations need more operating information than management accounts can provide. Older systems may not be capable of providing this information in a timely or cost-effective manner; they may not be capable of recording the base data in the first place.

To work around these problems, some organisations have used spreadsheets or databases to retain and manipulate this data. The problem with this solution is that the data extraction may be lengthy. The raw data may have to be re-keyed thus introducing duplicated effort. Also, the possibility for errors is magnified with each additional data transfer.

By installing an integrated suite of software, the core data need only be entered once. The data can be validated once only, at the point of entry. The operational system should be capable of retaining an immense amount of data, but only that data relevant to a particular business question need be extracted for further analysis.

In some ways, the installation of new systems will see a change of role for IS departments. Currently, one of the main concerns of IS managers is systems stability. This concern should diminish with the introduction of new systems; new systems are more fault tolerant and stable.

Instead the role of the IS Department will be to help to provide information to the business. The users may well design the reports; they may also write some of the reports. However, they will need the expertise of IS personnel to advise them where to find the raw data they need. The old job of bespoking systems in the background will move to the creation of new means of capturing and storing data. It should mean the creation of new methods of reporting back to management on business performance.

This change in role must be accompanied by the core operational systems being stable and secure. No longer will they need to be frequently replaced by new systems to provide more information. Whether the operational systems are character based (i.e. DOS) or GUI based (i.e. Windows) is irrelevant. What is important is that the core operational systems are capable of capturing the basic information that the business needs.

This information has two main functions:

1   to support other operational functions – the supplying of goods or services to customers and then ensuring that the customer pays you

2   to be summarised and manipulated into meaningful strategic information, to be used by the executive to assess how the business is performing overall.

A good robust core is needed for this. It must be functional and robust; it should be capable of enhancement and refinement. It must be able to cope with the growth and development of the business, but it need not be infinitely flexible or modifiable. It would be better to move to a newer product if the basic core no longer supports the operational side of the business.

By installing an integrated suite of programs, your business should now have a stable core. This stable core should be portable to newer systems when necessary.

Quicker Reporting

Modern systems will normally come with a powerful report writer capability. This means that the limitations of how information is entered may be overcome. For example, you may find that to give meaningful reports, you will need to combine information about both orders and invoices.

You could ask the software house to customise the orders programs to record this information. However, this additional information may already be recorded on the sales ledger. If so, then you could have a report written using the report writer to provide this information. This would remove the need to bespoke the package to suit your organisation's specific needs, and is a much cheaper solution.

The management could then decide how often this report is needed. If the information must be current then a powerful report writer might be needed. However, if a previous-day picture is sufficient then a report writer may be purchased for a minimal cost, say £2,000 for a sixteen-user licence.

Reports may be displayed and recorded in a number of ways: to screen, to paper, to disc, to fax or archived to CD-ROM. These reports may also be used to populate data in the data warehouse.

If you are installing more than one software package then you may be able to choose a report writer that will extract information from *all* the packages. This will reduce training time; it should also reduce the time taken to write new reports.

To summarise, improve management information as follows:

- use report writers to extract information;

- run reports for business critical information;

- run overnight batch reports;

- have improved daily control over entry of transactions.

Improved Quality of Information

Report writers should enable the data held on the database to be interrogated quickly and easily.

Setting up a number of daily exception reports to validate the information is a cost-effective way of ensuring the integrity of the data. Although new systems come with improved data validation checks, transpositions during input may still occur, or a valid code for an incorrect transaction may still be accepted. Simple standard overnight batch reports that search for any inconsistencies will ensure that the quality of the information is maintained. It is then easy to remedy these problems the next day, rather than some months later when some inconsistencies in senior management reports are noticed.

One of the justifications stated earlier was to reduce duplicated input; this benefit may be lost if time has to be spent later correcting erroneously entered data.

To summarise:

• information in reports should be more reliable;

• less time should be spent validating information in reports;

• there should be fewer inconsistencies.

Easier Extraction of Information

Using the report writer you can create ASCII files of data, which may allow you to overcome any data dictionary restrictions within report writers. Relationships may exist between the various data files holding the database information; those can be 'one to many' or 'many to one' relationships, and this affects how data can be accessed. Sometimes, using the standard files, you cannot capture all the data you need in one initial report; to overcome this you may have to 'build' intermediate files of data. This will be an extra cost to be noted. In a modern report writer, though, it is a straightforward exercise to create your own data files.

IS resources may be used to create information to run the business. However, the expertise in creating reports could easily be transferred to end user departments, and this would free up IS time and also empower end users to provide some of their own information.

These reports may be run as batch jobs each night, but this will mean that they will contain all transactions up to the close of business the previous day.

To summarise:

- add ASCII files to existing package database;

- load data into spreadsheets or databases for analysis purposes;

- download masterfile data and change key fields when business reorganising;

- make reorganising business simpler, by using software that may be modified rapidly to take account of restructuring.

Data Warehousing

One of the more recent buzz words in the literature has been data warehousing: the storage of vast quantities of transaction data in one central database. This information is then reported on to give a competitive edge to the business. Only recently, one of the top four supermarket groups has announced the development of a data warehouse.

Businesses are recognising that IS, used imaginatively, are able to do more than process routine transactions very quickly.

- They can also provide the ability to report rapidly on business performance and so trends should be discernible sooner, which should make the company more profitable.

- Data may be collected and collated for analytical purposes faster; this should enable the business to be more pro-active towards the marketplace.

- Potential stock outs or over capacity should be seen sooner. This should enable management to react to opportunities and respond to problems quicker.

- An analysis of this information should enable the business to understand its customer base. Recently, one large retail organisation considered dropping a dairy product. The sales of this product were not spectacular and the space could have been used for a more popular dairy item. However, analysis of purchasing patterns revealed that the majority of customers who used this retail location and spent over £100, bought this item. Through dropping this item, these customers might have shopped elsewhere, so the dairy product stayed on the shelves.

The trend towards data warehousing may also have been assisted by the growth of separate systems within organisations that have grown up around specific functions, e.g. sales systems or stock control systems. By combining this data in one database, the information may be cut many different ways. However, the data will need key fields to link all these transactions together. For example, the stock transactions must be linked in some way to the customer's order number held on the sales system.

The installation of new software is an ideal opportunity to standardise and rationalise coding within an organsiation. If not, then the data will have to be regrouped prior to entry into the data warehouse. This adds another step in the process with attendant cost and validation rules.

So, to summarise, you can

* gain competitive edge;

* process leads, quotes and orders more quickly;

* spot market trends sooner;

* identify problems earlier.

How to Measure the Value of Improved Management Information

This chapter, and the two following, examine potential improvements to your organisation. They focus on qualities that your organisation does not currently enjoy. To gain these qualities may involve a considerable investment. Your justification should therefore state the value to the business that the investment will produce. However, to try to put a value on these benefits will be difficult; there will be no hard evidence on which to base your conclusions, and so the value will be subjective.

In the previous three chapters, it has been possible to be fairly objective. While you may disagree with the percentage estimates used in the example in Appendix J, you should have, within your own organisation, enough knowledge and historical cost information to establish figures that will be appropriate to your own business.

Quicker Reporting

This improvement should enable management to monitor the business more closely. Any time delay in producing information currently should reduce. This should mean that management has more up-to-date information on which to base business decisions.

It should give management the facility to foresee opportunities sooner. It should also enable potential problem areas to be identified sooner and thus enable corrective action to be taken, before a problem escalates into a crisis.

Improved Quality of Information

The quality of information should be improved. There should be less need to verify what the information is reporting. Management should be able to take action on what is presented to them immediately, rather than ask for further clarification.

Think of Pareto's Law: 20% of your clients will provide 80% of your turnover.

Investment in IS may enable you to identify those important clients in the 20%. It might also help you to understand more clearly what they do want and what they do not need. How much would this information be worth to your business? I would suggest, quite a lot.

Easier Extraction of Information

For those areas of the business where information is insufficiently refined then relevant transaction data should be capable of being rapidly downloaded into whatever format managers prefer.

Managers may then manipulate and study the data using their preferred software package.

They should be able to analyse the data more effectively and to look at various scenarios and perform 'What if?' analyses.

Data Warehousing

The facility to build a data warehouse containing masses of easily manipulated data should enable the business to gain a competitive edge. Current trading patterns and levels should be capable of rapid analysis in many different ways. The data warehouse should be populated with useful data; this means that the greater part of the transaction data could be left behind in the core systems.

Departments could have access to this information through a database manipulation tool. This would enable users to interrogate in whatever way they wish. This would also free them from having to ask IS for assistance to write these enquiries. This should both empower users and free up IS staff time.

All of these benefits should, in theory, be translated into improvements in business performance.

7   Intangible benefits

This chapter considers various intangible benefits that may used in conjunction with those discussed in earlier chapters, to support the justification for investing in IS. As in the previous chapter, it is difficult to apply a specific monetary value to them. However, without them, the organisation would clearly suffer.

Improved Morale

If the implementation of new IS is presented as a positive action then staff morale tends to improve. It is essential to ensure that users' expectations are managed. If promised benefits are not delivered then users grow cynical and ignore the improvements made by the new systems. Thus, providing the users' expectations are managed, the expenditure should have a beneficial impact.

The change should be presented as broadening the skills base of staff – in effect, making them more marketable.

To summarise:

- staff will recognise that the organisation is investing in the future;

- the staff will see opportunities to learn new skills.

Motivated and Efficient Work Force

Through improving morale, end users should be more motivated to perform their jobs. This should increase productivity if they are provided with better tools to do their jobs.

Therefore:

- staff should see the benefits of a common system;

- implementation should ensure a common language within the organisation;

- the aim should be to reduce confusion and misunderstandings.

Flexible Staff

The introduction of standard organisation-wide systems should enable the development of multi-skilled end users. The end users should be more mobile and adaptable within the organisation. With standard company-wide systems, they should need less retraining on basic operating skills if they change departments.

To summarise:

- common systems should enable staff to be re-deployed at times of critical activity;

- minimal software retraining will be needed when people change departments;

- staff should understand and be more amenable to job or function changes;

- it should be easier to recruit trained staff when using common business software.

Valuation of Intangible Benefits

All organisations today need staff that help their boss; making an investment in IS is one method of equipping staff to help. The valuation of these intangible benefits is highly subjective. It is possible to see how they occur, and to see how they would benefit your organisation. You must be the best judge as to how much this investment could benefit your organisation:

In Appendix J, savings of 1–3% on general administration costs have been assumed.

Improved Morale

Content and motivated staff will have less time off for sickness. There should be a lower staff turnover. They should be more productive. They should work better together as a team, so the business unit should be more cohesive.

Motivated and Efficient Work Force

A shared understanding of the business objectives and priorities should arise among staff. They should be involved and committed to speeding up business processes.

Flexible Staff

In times of business pressure, it should be possible to redirect staff to those tasks that are crucial to the business. This should provide a ready pool of skilled staff available to tackle peaks in business activity.

8   Gateway to the future

Another business justification for investing in new IS is to open a gateway to the future. It is an opportunity to leave behind legacy systems and migrate to a modern stable platform. This should mean that the business is then equipped with systems capable of being easily upgraded in the future. This does not simply mean being tied to later versions of the same product. If necessary, it should be possible to migrate to a totally different platform.

To state clear specific business benefits in terms of future savings is not easy. However, these items are of definite benefit to the business. When preparing your business case they should be included as future benefits that will only become apparent when the need for them arises.

The installation of new systems today should mean that your data is improved in quality and consistency. Your processes should also have been re-designed, at least in part, to reflect the way IS now operate. This is not to imply that IS should be the driver. Rather the re-design of business processes should be part of a consensus-making process with the users.

One of the aftermaths of IS expenditure is that your business processes should now be documented and understood. This means that future consideration of new software platforms should be easier. To choose the next generation of software should be simpler!

Upgrade Path

One vital document that should have emerged during the production of a business case should be your IT strategy; this will have arisen out of the need to support the overall business strategy and should assist in designing and implementing changes to the IS for future needs.

These future developments should no longer be encumbered by legacy systems.

To summarise:

- the necessary steps to a successful implementation of new systems should mean that information is now portable – able to be loaded into newer releases of software applications;

- the business should be able to upgrade to new releases or bug fixes sooner.

Cheaper Enhancement

By moving to products with a wider installed base, it should be easier to obtain software improvements. Often, several users will recognise shortcomings in existing programs and they will seek improvements. None may have the financial resources to bespoke these changes, but, collective criticism to the software house may result in changes.

However, it may be necessary to resort to some bespoke programs because the requirements of your organisation demand special consideration.

In some instances, user groups may exist. These forums sometimes degenerate into whinging sessions in front of your peers; other groups may be more constructive, and will try to forge a working partnership between vendor and user.

Some software houses have a policy of incorporating bespoke work into later version releases of the standard software.

Briefly, then:

- as business needs change, software should be capable of developing with the business;

- often, specialist software companies are available to write specific add-ons;

- it can be easier to customise software to meet your business's specific needs.

Ease of Reorganising Core Information in Database

No business is static. No organisational structure lasts forever. At times of change, the business may demand that the way data is held be changed. The coding structure may need to be replaced to incorporate the new structure. Alternatively, specific items within the database may need amending. The facility to download data, manipulate into a new format and then reload may be very useful.

These changes could probably be made manually. However when there are, say, 20,000 records to change, this facility may be very beneficial to the business.

Briefly, then:

- modern software allows you to download master file data and change key fields if necessary;

- there is no need to purchase a licence to programming software;

- modern packages should have full data import menus.

Value of a Gateway to the Future

Upgrade Path

The costs of future migrations should be significantly less. This will be because the underlying business structures should now be in place. The IS should be in a position to support and enhance the business.

Cheaper Enhancement

The future developments of the new systems should be cheaper. It may be possible to steer through necessary changes with other users. Possibly, the costs of these changes may be shared with other users who need similar functionality.

Ease of Reorganising Core Information in Database

This facility should make restructuring of data quicker and more effective. It should enable the business to be rapidly reformed in times of business change.

9   Fixed costs of IS expenditure

This chapter, and the next, focus on a discussion of the potential costs involved in IS expenditure. The focus in Chapter 10 is primarily on uncertain costs as these are both harder to predict and contain; this chapter discusses aspects of fixed costs.

Hardware

On the choice of hardware, it is advisable to standardise on a recognised brand name. While it is possible to purchase clone PCs for less money than brand names – and your colleagues may offer advice on exactly what to purchase – when you are supporting ten or more PCs, any initial savings can soon be outweighed by support problems.

Support problems can be exacerbated by certain software products, each brand of PC has its quirks. At least by standardising on one brand you reduce the number of quirks to which you become exposed. You should also have access to a much larger support organisation for resolving problems, and this should also translate into reduced maintenance costs.

Networked PCs and their file servers should have a useful life of about four years. By not buying branded products, you may save, say, £300 per unit initially. That amounts to roughly £4 per week over the product's working life. If you have to spend two days trying to solve a problem on a rogue PC then you have soon spent double that amount.

Backup devices such as tape streamers transfer data from the hard disc onto tape for storage. Again, these should be standard across all your platforms. In the event of one breaking down, you may simply remove the tape device from one machine and install it into another. This interchangeability will save time and grief later. If you miss a backup, that will be the one you need later!

The advantage of printer network points is that network printers may be accessed independently of a host PC. Without this hardware, when the PC connected to the printer is turned off, the printer may not be used, and as luck would have it the very time users want to print something extremely urgent is just when the person who knows the password to that PC has gone home.

Core Business Software

The choice of solution should be driven by suitability to match business needs, and this should be driven by the IT strategy of the organisation. These are factors to weigh in the choice:

- **Installed base**

  How many organisations are currently using the software? The width of the installed base of established products may provide an indicator as to the quality of the software. (This may not be true of recent releases...) Do the types of organisation using the software match your business?

- **Current release version**

  How established is the software? What is the release version?

- **Benchmarking results**

  You may be able to obtain reports from technical publications that measure similar types of software. How does the software compare?

- **Cost**

  How much is the software? What is the price for a set number of users?

- **Business fit**

  Does the software solution support your IS strategy and hence your business strategy?

- **Adaptability**

  How flexible is the software? Would it be relatively inexpensive to tailor to your business needs?

- **Support costs**

  What are the annual telephone support costs? How much extra would it cost to have someone on site?

- **Installation costs**

  How long should installation take? What disruption will there be to the business?

Office Software

There are a number of competing products available for desktop work. It makes sense to source these from one supplier; the advantages of this approach are compatibility and familiarity in use.

There are also on the market some inexpensive add ons which considerably enhance both office software and core business software. These useful utilities may offer inexpensive solutions to operating difficulties identified with the core systems.

Briefly then, look for:

- single source for e-mail, word processing and spreadsheets;

- useful utilities;

- software installation.

Fixtures and Fittings

At first sight, this may seem an unnecessary additional expense. After all, your staff already have desks and chairs. However, health and safety legislation concerning the use of computers is becoming much stricter, so this may well be a good opportunity to ensure that staff using VDUs have proper workstations.

Fixtures and fittings include:

- computer room

- desks

- foot rests

- chairs

- swivel arms

- fire proof safe

- stationery.

Network Installation

These items comprise the hardware necessary to set up a local area network (LAN).

- Network points

- Network cards

- Ethernet cable (or similar)

- Repeaters

- Network software

- Network installation

Network Software

These items of software are necessary to access the PCs and the software installed on the network.

- Network software

- Virus checking software

- Network protocol software

10 Uncertain costs of IS expenditure

Uncertain costs are much harder to predict than those listed in Chapter 9. Some costs will only become apparent as the implementation proceeds; others may increase or decrease as the implementation progresses. You may encounter unexpected problems that must be solved, but, the investment of time initially, in evaluation and planning, should allow you to identify most potential problem areas.

How do you decide which system to choose? You may have justified the business case for replacing existing systems. However, there is a plethora of competing hardware and software products from which to choose. One of the simplest guides is to establish your overall budget. Do not simply tot up hardware and software costs; these will probably amount to no more than 50% of what you will actually have to spend. The rest of the spend will be on some or all of the items listed here.

You may be tempted to spend less on what seem like peripheral items, such as training and running a project team. This is inadvisable – you will need to involve the end users throughout if they are to accept the chosen solution. You will also need the support of management to ensure that changes in business processes necessary for success are implemented.

Initial Systems Evaluation Prior to Purchase

Once you have narrowed your choice down to, say, three competing products from the trade magazines, salesmen and peer groups, you will need to evaluate the product. The more embracing the implementation then the more time you will need to devote to this stage. However, it is important to establish early on what the software can and cannot do.

You could employ a consultancy to evaluate your three choices. The consultancy could prepare a report covering areas in which you lack expertise. There is very little use in their simply reciting the functionality of the software only. What you are looking for is a comparison between the alternatives and a recommendation. You will need advice on recommended hardware platforms, upgradability, numbers in use, etc.

You should visit sites where the software is actually being used. These live users will often give a candid, but not necessarily damming, report on how the software works in practice. Existing users may enlighten you on points that will not have occurred to you as a new user.

For major software releases, the trade publications will carry reviews. These publications should provide you with background information to the products of interest to you, and often these reports will attempt some form of benchmarking. You should also be able to obtain back copies of these.

The costs involved in this evaluation will depend upon just how much you are prepared to spend: the longer you spend, the greater the cost.

To summarise, you need to include costs of:

- consultancy

- site visits

- reports.

Bespoke Software

Having identified the limitations of the software you propose to purchase, you may well find that some features are missing. This is software functionality deemed necessary by your organisation but missing from the software that you propose to purchase. It may be possible, through a change in business procedures, to remove the need for these changes. In some instances though this functionality must be incorporated into the IS.

You will then be confronted with two choices. Do you bespoke the package software? Or do you have separate programs written that operate independently of the main package? This is a tricky decision to make.

The advantage of having the original package bespoked is that *all* the software support is passed to the one supplier. The disadvantage is that this may tie you to the current version, or at the very least mean that the bespoke has to be redone before you can upgrade. This aspect is worth careful consideration, especially if one of your justifications was to open an upgrade path.

Alternatively, you could commission specially written add-on software programs. This extra software could take data feeds from your main package; it might also be possible to feed data back – and this would require some links to exist or to be written. The bulk of the processing, though, would be done independently of the main software. The advantage of this option is that, when you choose to upgrade, only the links would need to be rewritten. The disadvantage is that this element of software would be unique to your company, which may have implications for system support; it may prove expensive to maintain in the long term.

Another problem with choosing the bespoking route, irrespective of whether it is done within or outside the package, is that users may come to expect it as the automatic solution to any shortfall in the software. Any minor anomaly within the proposed system may then be held to make the software unworkable – unless, of course, it is changed. This is a very slippery slope! It is at least worth considering whether it would be better (i.e. less expensive and more sensible) to amend a business process rather than to attempt to change the software.

It is necessary to test any new software. A test programme should be drawn up, which should be agreed by users. Then, rigorous testing should occur. Even in this Utopian environment, the test programme may be deficient, and situations may occur live which were overlooked. Thus when the system goes live, new problems may occur while the bespoke software is bedded in. How damaging this may be to the business depends in part on how soon any problems are spotted. The earlier bugs are identified then the sooner the software may be fixed. Later, there may be more rectification work needed to recover the situation.

The cost of any bespoke work needs to be carefully matched to the benefit to the business.

To summarise,

•   costs can be ongoing to allow upgradability

•   consequential problems may occur, e.g. support

•   it can be difficult to control if users' demands are *always* met.

Setting Up and Testing the New Systems

The advantages of having a separate test system cannot be over-emphasised. Ideally, it should not be populated with dummy data supplied by the software house. Instead, use your own data, in the format that your organisation uses. This makes testing so much simpler. The reason? You are familiar with the transactions.

To test new hardware and/or software you need to transfer data from the old systems onto the new. For new software, this may involve considerable effort in cleaning up your existing data before you can load it onto the new software. This data cleaning and data transfer may amount to significant cost. This will be especially true if you are merging data previously held on several separate databases, e.g. if you were merging data from sales, stock control and finance onto one package.

It is well worth hiring an extra machine for this period. You should set up the system so that the transaction files are stored regularly. This means, if need be, that you can retry all the software routines. Then, when something happens that you are unsure of, you can stop and restore the earlier versions of the data files. Then you can run the software routines again. Having a distinct and separate test environment prevents you from accidentally damaging live data, and the performance of the live system should not be degraded.

It is not a good idea to try to work out of hours on your existing hardware. This practice is likely to terminate relationships and friendships both within and outside the business. While employees may be willing to stay behind a couple of times to train, it is unreasonable to ask them to spend their own time on training. If you do, they will assure you that they need no more training! It is much better to test any new system using current staff during the normal working day.

You could employ additional temporary staff to assist with some of the testing; for specific discrete areas, this can be a reasonable approach. You do need to decide what the expected test results should be. Otherwise, a temp might assume that what the system produces is correct.

You could pay more for a highly paid consultant with a wider range of experience, hoping this knowledge may assist in concluding the test phase sooner.

A more imaginative and constructive use of temporary staff is for them to do the jobs of existing staff. This then frees existing staff to test and train on the new systems. The best judge of the functionality of software is not the Project Manager or Finance Director, but the end user. Whether their complaints are acted on, is a matter for the Project Manager or Finance Director. However, the identification of these problems should be done by the end user.

It is probably as easy to write this as it is hard to get it implemented in practice.

Even the finance people – accountants and bookkeepers – have their uses during the testing phase. All financial data should be reconciled and any new procedures set up at this stage. You must not let Finance wait till you go live. Otherwise on day nine, just when you are starting to relax, they will appear and say: 'We've noticed something odd ...'

Costs to consider in this phase include:

- configuration of the test environment

- data cleaning prior to data transfer

- data transfers

- temporary staff and consultants.

Remember that:

- testing may need to be done out of hours

- financial data must be reconciled vigorously and vigilantly.

Business Disruption

You may be making a major system change, and think that because of your meticulous planning and testing everything is covered. Be prepared for a stressful time!

Day one ends, and everything is quiet on the software front in the Stock Control front-line. Day two opens with the 'bug offensive'. Do you remember all the testing that was done? When you asked if there were any other scenarios that you should test, didn't they all just shake their heads from side to side? Well, Andy in Stores has just spotted a major howler.

Day seven. You are ready to begin day one again.

Day three in Sales: 'We've been doing it this way since Monday. Why has it stopped working?' Probably, you think, they have just turned all the outstanding quotes into cash orders. 'Oh, is that why all those delivery trucks are round the back of the warehouse?'

There is bound to be a fall in productivity while users become more comfortable with the new systems. Often this is because operators will slow down to a speed with which they feel comfortable. The number of orders processed for example will fall due to this unfamiliarity. Plan for it. Monitor it. If the learning curve is too flat then consider further training. Also, look at how they are using the software. Has the business process been reformed for the new software?

Mistakes will be made. Items may well have to be re-entered twice. If you have the right controls in place then this should not run to hundreds of items. The aim is to try to identify the problem areas early.

Once again the use of temporary staff should be considered. If you are moving to a more standard platform then you may be able to hire staff familiar with the software. This should only be a temporary hiccup. Rather than pressurise staff too much, it might be worth giving them a temporary boost.

These are the specific items to consider during this stage:

- Inadequate testing may mask bugs that only become apparent when you go live.

- The cost of the learning curve – business productivity will fall in the short term.

- Deside where to make best use of temporary staff.

- Take time to manage awkward staff.

Skills Profile for New IS Staff

This section discusses the additional training of existing staff and the recruitment of staff with the new skills necessary to use the new systems.

With the introduction of both new hardware or software, management need to decide what skills profile will be necessary to support the new IS. In essence, decisions will have to be made about who to train and on what.

If part of the IT strategy is to move towards out-sourcing then a clear dividing line will need to be decided between those skills to retain in-house and those you plan to out-source. As discussed in Chapter 2, this may reduce systems maintenance costs. The key is to ensure that the business always has adequate cover.

To establish clearly what cover is needed, a Service Level Agreement between the IS Department and the business managers of the organisation needs to be agreed. This document should cover areas such as agreed downtime. How long should pass before faults on the system should be fixed? It should also state clearly who is responsible for which parts of the systems. Are the users responsible for monitoring the data integrity and quality of their information?

Without these guidelines it will prove impossible to establish what additional training is necessary and what new skills are needed.

Another area to consider is exactly when to train staff on the new systems. Ideally, this should be ongoing for IS throughout the implementation, but for end users, this should occur in the period immediately prior to going live. However, the business still needs to function and this may mean that the training has to occur earlier; the drawback of this is that users may be rusty by the time they go live. Timing of training is a management decision; IS should provide a reasoned recommendation, and may thus persuade the management to provide additional resources to enable the training to occur at the optimum time.

You may decide that it is inappropriate to retrain some existing staff. The skills profile will enable you to decide the skills you need from new employees to support the new systems. The existence of a defined skills list should make looking for candidates easier. There are numerous recruitment agencies. All you need to do is to circulate them with your requirements. By recruiting new staff, you also have the opportunity to assess them on the job. If they are not capable of doing the work then it is easier to replace them.

If you intend to reduce staff numbers through the implementation, then you will need to consider the matter of redundancy. This is not just a matter of the cost. The legislation today is complex and should be adhered to. The cost of redundancy should also be included in the costings for the new systems.

In summary, you need to consider:

- how much training to provide

- to whom

- the type of training – cascade or everyone?

- when to train: now or just before going live (testing) or after going live (testing)?

- who to recruit

- what skills profile company needs now

- the redundancy costs.

Creation of Business Processes Documentation

Too often, only the functionality of the new software is considered. Does it have a sales ledger? Yes. Does it handle stock? Yes. Will it handle purchasing? Yes. Can we afford it? Too little consideration is given to how the software fits together overall. Does it fit the overall business strategy? Will it actually benefit your organisation?

By having documentation for existing business processes, it is easy to evaluate what impact the proposed new software will have on business processes. Will people's jobs and responsibilities need to change? Will the software do what the business needs? Ideally, this documentation should exist prior to the evaluation stage. Does the software address the core needs of the business? For example, does it assist Finance at the expense of hampering Sales? This needs to be established early on. What operational impact will implementing these systems have on the business?

Often, within organisations, existing documentation is sketchy and incomplete. If so, then these processes should be reviewed and documented during the evaluation stage. At least this way management may be forewarned that businesses processes may need to change to accommodate the new software. If the management considers that these changes are too disruptive, then a different software solution may be needed. It is vital to establish this early on. Otherwise, the full benefits will not be reaped when the IS go live.

For example, earlier in the justification stage, we discussed one of the benefits as being the reduction of duplication. However, if business processes are not reformed to remove this duplication then it will probably be replicated unnecessarily on the new systems. Without the establishment of clear business procedures and responsibilities, the hoped-for efficiencies will not occur.

Items that should be documented include:

- flow charts of business processes

- process charts of organisation

- organisational structure

- charts showing department responsibilities for specific software functions.

Creation and Maintenance of IS Documentation

To ensure that the new systems are stable, the operational procedures of the new systems need to be fully documented. This will have to be an in-house document covering all aspects of the systems that are the responsibility of the IS department.

The procedures should cover all aspects of the systems. It should cover all daily, weekly, monthly and annual procedures. In effect, it should be an 'idiot's guide'. It should cover all aspects of IS maintenance: from data backup procedures to major data restores in the event of corruption of the database. Only with this documentation may you be confident that IS staff and end users will control the software effectively.

No matter how qualified and how well trained, staff will at times make mistakes. Normally the greater the sense of urgency or the greater the crisis, the more likely a mistake will be made. What you should have, are clear instructions to be followed in any foreseeable eventuality. This is not a five-minute job. Once these procedures are recorded, they will need to be maintained and updated.

The benefit though is that when a situation arises, staff should have a guide:

-            In this instance, do this.

-            If this fails, then do this.

-            If this fails, then contact X.

What you want to reduce is inspired initiative in times of crisis; this is when procedures must be followed to the letter. Otherwise you may get a snowball effect: one wrong action leads to another. This detailed documentation will also save precious time during the annual audit.

The following processes are illustrations of what should be documented:

-            Backup procedures

-            How restores of data from backup should be done

-            Flow charts of information systems

-            Narrative to explain flow charts

-            Register of all hardware

-            Register of all software

Unforeseen Contingencies

No matter how meticulous your planning and preparation, something unforeseen will occur during the course of the implementation. It may arise from internal pressures. It may be caused by factors beyond your control. Some provision within your costing should allow for this. In the worked example in Appendix H an estimate of 5% of the total project cost has been allowed to provide for unforeseen contingencies.

As an example, I was about to upgrade the RAM memory chips in a considerable number of PCs when a fire in Japan destroyed 40% of the manufacturing capacity for RAM chips. As a consequence, the price of the chips shot up and I had to delay the upgrade until prices had fallen.

Examples of unforeseen contingencies include:

- testing takes longer than planned

- additional bespoke software required to ensure specification matches business needs

- rise in hardware prices

- loss of crucial staff.

Regular Systems Implementation Reviews

Throughout the course of the implementation, senior management will need to set aside regular time slots to review progress. Management must be prepared to contribute this time. It means that the costs of this time must be budgeted for. This is necessary to see that the project is on time and delivering the expected benefits.

Without this formal review process, it is easy for 'scope drift' to set in. The original goal posts are turned into a moving target – the project will never achieve its original target, and users may become disillusioned.

The review process serves to ensure that the implementation is kept focused and on target.

You need to consider the following:

- costs of the steering group

- frequency of regular review meetings

- the composition of steering group.

11 Capital investment appraisal of IS expenditure

Introduction

The costing of IS expenditure may be broken down into three main areas.

1   Capital investment analysis

2   the impact on the company's published accounts and

3   the impact on corporation tax payable by the company.

Capital investment analysis is a method of assessing whether the investment in IS that the company is proposing to make will actually benefit the company. By benefit, I mean will the future efficiencies and additional sales generated, exceed or cover the proposed expenditure on IS?

This calculation will obviously depend in part on the accuracy of the figures prepared in the justification. To try to ensure that the original estimates are reasonably accurate I recommend preparing three sets of costings: low, medium and high. This way you may illustrate both the best and the worst case scenarios.

Methods of Calculating

There are a number of different methods of calculating whether a proposed investment has a positive or negative impact on a business's profits. Probably the simplest to use is **discounted cash** flows. This approach is widely used within business. Although it is not the only method, it will provide a clear indication of whether the investment is a good or bad idea.

If necessary, more sophisticated models may be built. However, this method is sufficient for a first pass to establish whether it is worth proceeding further.

Discounted Cash Flows

This method focuses on cash flows, rather than accounting profits – money out of your bank account and money into your bank account – and the cash flow implications of the proposed expenditure.

This considerably simplifies the matter as it removes the evaluation from the world of accounting conventions. In brief, it should show whether or not the project is worth it and how long it will take for the project to pay for itself. This method recognises the time value of money: a pound today is worth more than a pound in one year's time.

What is Net Present Value?

This method calculates in present day money terms whether the expected future cost savings through IS expenditure will exceed both the initial cost of putting in the systems in the first place and maintaining them for a number of years.

Basically, you need to prepare a schedule showing:

- what the costs are

- the dates when the organisation will have to pay out these costs

- what the expected cost savings will be

- the dates when these expected cost savings should occur.

Requirements for Calculating Net Present Value (NPV)

A sample calculation of NPV is given in Appendix M.

Five elements are needed to calculate NPV.

Cost of capital

This may be taken as the rate at which the bank will lend money to your company for a given period of time. The current bank base rate may be used as an initial starting point. Or you could use the rate at which your bank currently lends money to your organsiation. In Appendix M, a current bank rate of 6.0% is used.

Payback Period

This is the number of years over which the benefits of the IS expenditure should accrue to the organisation. This should be apparent from the schedule prepared earlier. For the purposes of Appendix M the savings are assumed to be spread over four years.

Initial Investment

The amount of initial investment in setting up the IS should also be included in the schedule.

Expected Future Savings

These are the expected future savings that are anticipated to result from the IS investment.

Future Investment Needs

This is the amount of future investment needed to maintain the systems.

Sensitivity Analysis

The values reported in the NPV calculation may be further refined using sensitivity analysis. This means weighting the variables involved.

How likely are you to run over time during testing? You could establish a low estimate as 0.2, a medium estimate as 0.5 and a high estimate as 0.3. You would then multiply the costs to arrive at an expected value. The problem here is in deciding what the probability is.

The costs of such an exercise may well outweigh the benefits.

12 Company taxation of IS expenditure

Introduction

As a general rule, hardware and software purchases may be capitalised. The term capitalised means the purchases are not charged immediately to the profit and loss account for the year in which the expenditure is incurred. In effect this means that the cost of acquiring computer hardware and software must be spread over a number of years. However, there are two basic accountancy rules with which you should be familiar. These are the **prudence** and **consistency** concepts.

Prudence Concept

Accountancy theory adopts a pessimistic approach. When forecasting into the future, always look on the dark side. What do you realistically expect the future life of your IS investment to be. Ten years? Two years? Your accountant will ask you to state the minimal useful life that you expect from your hardware or software.

The number of years should be the shortest estimate of the useful life of the software. Although new software is constantly hitting the market place when you consider the sums involved in IS expenditure then I do not think that four years is an unreasonable estimate for the useful life of a new piece of software.

Consistency Concept

Accountants also prefer that a company adopt a consistent approach to the capitalisation of computer hardware and software. If the stated policy in your company accounts was to capitalise hardware but to write of all software immediately to the Profit and Loss Account in the year of purchase, it is advisable to keep to this practice. Do not decide to capitalise software in year three just because you have had a poor year's trading.

If you are able to make a convincing case for a change in policy then your previous years' accounts may have to be restated. This may then in turn attract the interest of the Corporation Tax authorities. They may then ask for tax on your restated higher earnings for previous years.

Thus it is worth deciding at the outset what your organisation's accounting treatment will be of hardware and software investment. You may wish to discuss this with your auditors before making a final decision.

Proof of Ownership and Existence

To satisfy your auditors and the Inland Revenue that you actually possess the items that you propose to capitalise, you need to prepare a register of all hardware and software that you purchase.

This register should already be in existence through your IS documentation.

What to Capitalise

The choice of what to capitalise is partly down to you. The ceiling on when you must capitalise is not defined in value. The rules look at the nature of the asset. Is it a capital item? The definitions are fairly clear. If the item is something that would not be resold in the normal course of business then it should be capitalised. However, small value items may be charged direct to the Profit and Loss Account. Small though, is dependent upon the size of your business.

The more expenditure you capitalise then the higher your earnings. This may appeal to your shareholders. However, the more the business earns then the more tax it will pay.

What element of software purchases may be capitalised is harder to define. You should be allowed the initial purchase cost of the software and any bespoke software. However, the annual support or licensing payment would not be allowable. Similarly, neither would items such as initial systems evaluation, business disruption or testing costs. Thus, during the financial year(s) in which the implementation is taking place, possibly significant extra costs will reduce the company's profits.

Reporting of Capitalised Information Expenditure in Published Accounts

In a company's accounts normally the first item is **fixed assets**, i.e. assets held by the company for use over a number of years. It is within this category that computer assets, both hardware and software, are recorded.

Under normal accounting practice, purchases consumed within one year are charged immediately to the Profit and Loss Account. Those purchases where the benefit is expected to last more than one year and the cost is significant, say £500 or above, are capitalised and only a portion of those costs are charged to the Profit and Loss Account. The accountancy term for the amount charged to the Profit and Loss Account each year is **depreciation**.

Companies often adopt straight-line depreciation for fixed assets. This means writing off an equal amount of the purchase price each year.

Example

Suppose you buy computer hardware in Year 1 costing £10,000.

If you depreciate over four years, these will be the charges to the Profit and Loss Account.

	Charge to the Profit and Loss Account	Balance Sheet Value
Year 1	£2,500	£7,500
Year 2	£2,500	£5,000
Year 3	£2,500	£2,500
Year 4	£2,500	£ Nil

13 Corporation taxation of IS expenditure

Introduction

Under the current Income Tax and Corporation Tax rules, allowance is made for capital expenditure under the heading of **Capital Allowances**. The general rule is that capital expenditure on hardware or software may be charged to the Profit and Loss Account at 25% per annum on the reducing balance method.

This rule applies irrespective of the type of organisation trading; it applies to public limited companies, private limited companies, partnerships and sole traders alike.

Example

Consider again the example from Chapter 12: buying computer hardware in Year 1 for £10,000.

In the accounts for Year 1, £2,500 (=25% of 10,000) would be allowed to be offset against profits. The net value of the item in the company's corporation tax workings would be £7,500 (=£10,000 − £2,500).

In the accounts for Year 2, £1,875 (=25% of 7,500) would be allowed. The net value of the item in the company's corporation tax workings would be £5,625 (=£7,500 − £1,875).

Thus the amount of the original expenditure that is allowable against tax for each financial year reduces. This means that the original expenditure will not be recovered until several years pass.

You will note that the amount allowed under Corporation Tax is different for that allowed to be charged to the company's Profit and Loss Account under accountancy rules. In effect, the company's accounts write off the asset sooner than the Corporation Tax allows.

Definition of Short-life Assets

Possibly, partly in recognition of the short life of computer equipment, the government introduced **short-life assets**. For specific named items, the company may elect to calculate the capital allowances for these items separately. This is known as an election to **de-pool** and should be made within two years of the purchase date.

Under Revenue Statement of Practice SP 1/86 where it is not practical to separately identify short-life assets they may be pooled. In effect, this means that items purchased in the same year may be put into the same capital allowances pool.

Short-life Assets Capital Allowances

In effect, these items – if sold within five years of purchase – are entitled to 100% of their capital allowances. Under the original rules, the company would have still had to continue claiming the capital allowances long after the items had been sold or scrapped.

At the end of the five-year period any items not disposed of are transferred to the general pool. The opportunity to claim the full allowances within five years is thus lost if the computer equipment is not disposed of within this period. However, the amounts remaining will probably not be too significant.

The advantage of electing to treat computer purchases as short-life assets is that, if the hardware or software rapidly becomes redundant, then tax benefits may be obtained for the full amount of the original cost.

The disadvantage is that separate pools (records) of each item have to be maintained. The use of a spreadsheet to record these items should mean that the task is not too onerous compared to the possible advantages.

Appendix A: Business case proposal form – investment in IS

Proposer	
Submitted by	C.Cooper
Date	15/5/96
Department	Marketing
Cost Centre Code	018-410

Sponser	
Reviewed by	J.Bosley
Approved (Y/N)	Y
Budget Hours	100
Budget Cost	£5,000

Information Systems	
Start Date	1/7/96
Completion Date	14/7/96

Priority Level	
Urgent	A
Necessary	B
Nice	C

Justification for the investment

What alternatives exist

Consequences of doing nothing

Other departments affected

Benefits of the expenditure

Costs of the expenditure

Appendix B: <u>Summary of total costs of typical implementation</u>

	Total Cost			Example of Accounting Treatment		
	Low £	Medium £	High £	Category	Capital £	Revenue £
Hardware	67,050	89,300	133,800	C	67,050	
Main financial/business software	79,200	100,600	143,200	C/R	68,000	11,200
Office software	15,175	15,175	15,175	C	15,175	
Fixtures & fittings	24,750	34,250	43,750	C	24,750	
Network installation	14,500	17,500	20,500	C	14,500	
Network software	9,000	9,000	9,000	C	9,000	
Total certain costs	209,675	265,825	365,425		198,475	11,200
Initial systems evaluation	6,300	7,200	8,100	R		6,300
Bespoke software	7,500	10,000	15,000	C	7,500	
Setting up and testing new systems	7,000	8,000	9,000	R		7,000
Business disruption	10,000	15,000	20,000	R		10,000
Additional training and recruitment	9,000	12,000	15,000	R		9,000
Creation of systems documentation	7,500	11,250	15,000	R		7,500
Testing enviroment	3,000	4,000	5,000	R		3,000
System reviews	10,000	10,000	10,000	R		10,000
Unforeseen contingencies	13,499	17,164	23,126	R		13,499
Total uncertain costs	73,799	94,614	120,226		7,500	66,299
TOTAL COSTS	283,474	360,439	485,651		205,975	77,499

Appendix C: Graph of total implementation costs

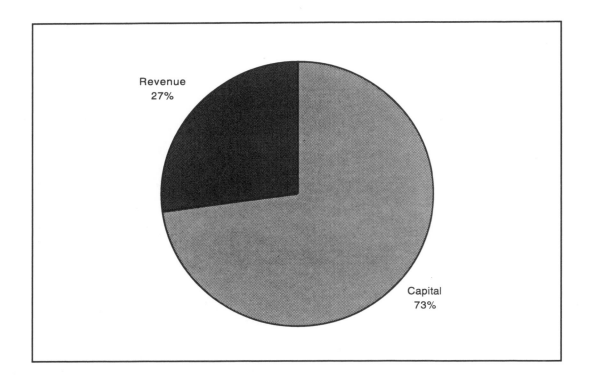

Appendix D: Graph of capital costs of implementation

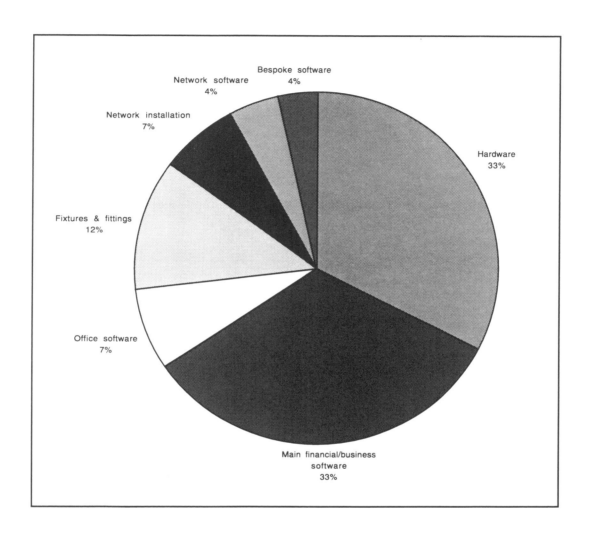

Appendix E: Graph of revenue costs of implementation

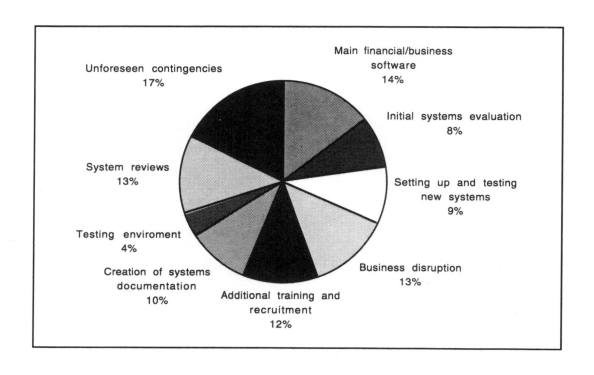

Main financial/business
software
14%

Unforeseen contingencies
17%

Initial systems evaluation
8%

System reviews
13%

Setting up and testing
new systems
9%

Testing enviroment
4%

Creation of systems
documentation
10%

Additional training and
recruitment
12%

Business disruption
13%

Appendix F: <u>Table of certain costs</u>

Sample Configuration of Fifty User Network System to Provide Benefits Listed in Justification

	Accounting Category	Qty	Unit Cost Low £	Unit Cost Medium £	Unit Cost High £	Total Cost Low £	Total Cost Medium £	Total Cost High £
Hardware								
Network file server	c	1	5,000	6,667	10,000	5,000	6,667	10,000
Operating Software file server	c	1	5,000	6,667	10,000	5,000	6,667	10,000
PCs	c	50	1,000	1,333	2,000	50,000	66,667	100,000
Backup devices	c	2	1,500	2,000	3,000	3,000	4,000	6,000
Printers + paper trays	c	4	750	1,000	1,500	3,000	4,000	6,000
Printer network ports	c	2	150	150	150	300	300	300
Installation of two servers in working days	c	2	375	500	750	750	1,000	1,500
						67,050	89,300	133,800
Main financial/business software								
Network software	c	50	250	250	250	12,500	12,500	12,500
Business software (**BS**)	c	50	1,000	1,333	2,000	50,000	66,667	100,000
Report writers (**RWs**)	c	20	150	200	300	3,000	4,000	6,000
Windows	c	50	50	50	50	2,500	2,500	2,500
Annual licensing for **BS**	R	20%	200	267	400	10,000	13,333	20,000
Annual support for **RWs**	R	20%	30	40	60	600	800	1,200
Attending user groups 4 per annum	R	8	75	100	125	600	800	1,000
						79,200	100,600	143,200
Office software								
Spreadsheets	c	20	200	200	200	4,000	4,000	4,000
Word processing	c	20	200	200	200	4,000	4,000	4,000
Databases	c	5	250	250	250	1,250	1,250	1,250
E-mail	c	50	50	50	50	2,500	2,500	2,500
Attending user groups	c	4	75	75	75	300	300	300
Useful utilities	c	5	250	250	250	1,250	1,250	1,250
Office software installation in working days	c	5	375	375	375	1,875	1,875	1,875
						15,175	15,175	15,175
Fixtures & fittings								
• Desks	c	50	150	200	250	7,500	10,000	12,500
• Chairs	c	50	50	75	100	2,500	3,750	5,000
• Foot rests	c	50	25	30	35	1,250	1,500	1,750
• Computer room	c	1	5,000	7,500	10,000	5,000	7,500	10,000
• Uninterrupted power supply	c	1	2,000	2,000	2,000	2,000	2,000	2,000
• Swivel arms	c	20	75	100	125	1,500	2,000	2,500
• Fire-proof safe	c	1	5,000	7,500	10,000	5,000	7,500	10,000
						24,750	34,250	43,750
Network Installation								
• Installation of network software in working da	c	5	375	375	375	1,875	1,875	1,875
• Wiring of network (ethernet cable)	c	5	375	375	375	1,875	1,875	1,875
• Repeaters	c	5	250	250	250	1,250	1,250	1,250
• Network cards in PCs	c	50	150	200	250	7,500	10,000	12,500
• Network points on walls	c	100	20	25	30	2,000	2,500	3,000
						14,500	17,500	20,500
Network software								
• Novell/NT software	c	50	100	100	100	5,000	5,000	5,000
• Additional network software	c	20	100	100	100	2,000	2,000	2,000
• Virus checking software	c	20	50	50	50	1,000	1,000	1,000
• Traffic monitoring software	c	20	50	50	50	1,000	1,000	1,000
						9,000	9,000	9,000
						209,675	265,825	365,425

Appendix G: <u>Graph of certain costs</u>

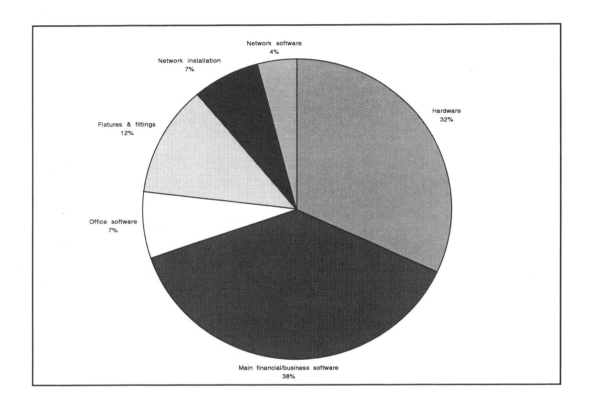

Appendix H: Table of uncertain costs

	%	Qty in Days	Unit Cost			Total Cost		
			Low £	Medium £	High £	Low £	Medium £	High £
Initial systems evaluation								
Consultancy		10	350	400	450	3,500	4,000	4,500
Site visits		4	350	400	450	1,400	1,600	1,800
Reports		4	350	400	450	1,400	1,600	1,800
Bespoke software								
Assumed at 15% of purchase price	15%		150	200	300	7,500	10,000	15,000
Setting up and testing new systems								
Assumed twenty working days		20	350	400	450	7,000	8,000	9,000
Business disruption								
Assumed one month learning curve of working days		20	500	750	1,000	10,000	15,000	20,000
Additional training and recruitment								
Assumed training & temporary staff necessary		60	150	200	250	9,000	12,000	15,000
Creation of systems documentation								
Assumed twenty working days		15	500	750	1,000	7,500	11,250	15,000
Testing enviroment								
Assumed twenty working days		20	150	200	250	3,000	4,000	5,000
System reviews								
Assumed project last 10 weeks		20	500	500	500	10,000	10,000	10,000
Unforeseen contingencies								
Assumed 5% of total project cost	5%					13,499	17,164	23,126
						73,799	**94,614**	**120,226**

Appendix I: Graph of uncertain costs

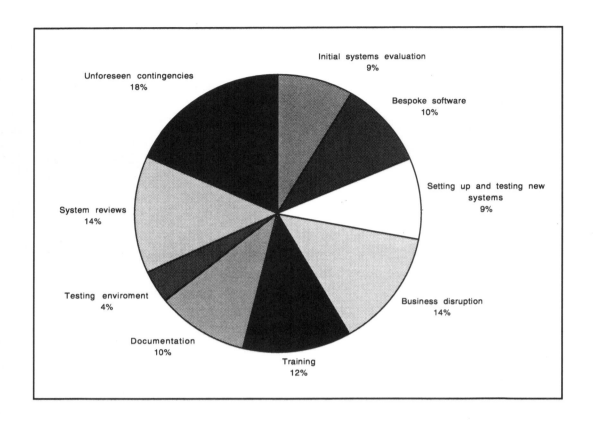

Initial systems evaluation
9%

Unforeseen contingencies
18%

Bespoke software
10%

Setting up and testing new systems
9%

System reviews
14%

Business disruption
14%

Testing enviroment
4%

Documentation
10%

Training
12%

Appendix J: Table of potential cost savings through investment in IS

Justification	Current spend per year	Possible improvements			Forecast savings per annum		
		Low	Medium	High	Low £	Medium £	High £
Improve business administration							
Improve business processes	400,000	3.00%	4.00%	5.00%	12,000	16,000	20,000
Business process re-engineering	400,000	5.00%	7.50%	10.00%	20,000	30,000	40,000
Integrated database	400,000	2.00%	3.00%	4.00%	8,000	12,000	16,000
Focus on main business	250,000	3.00%	4.00%	5.00%	7,500	10,000	12,500
					47,500	68,000	88,500
Save money on information systems							
Cheaper systems support	200,000	15.00%	20.00%	25.00%	30,000	40,000	50,000
Less reliant on specialist knowledge	100,000	20.00%	25.00%	30.00%	20,000	25,000	30,000
Out sourcing							
Fewer staff	100,000	10.00%	15.00%	20.00%	10,000	15,000	20,000
					60,000	80,000	100,000
Provide secure core systems							
Less down time	400,000	3.00%	4.00%	5.00%	12,000	16,000	20,000
Fewer data losses	400,000	0.50%	0.75%	1.00%	2,000	3,000	4,000
Improved security							
Use of packages allows							
					14,000	19,000	24,000
Improve management information							
Quicker reporting	250,000	5.00%	7.50%	10.00%	12,500	18,750	25,000
Improved quality of information	250,000	2.50%	5.00%	7.50%	6,250	12,500	18,750
Easier to extra to information	100,000	5.00%	7.50%	10.00%	5,000	7,500	10,000
Build data warehouse							
					23,750	38,750	53,750
Gateway to the future							
Upgrade path							
Cheaper to enhance	75,000	15.00%	20.00%	25.00%	11,250	15,000	18,750
Easier to reorganise/ upload data							
Investment in future							
					11,250	15,000	18,750
Intangible benefits							
Improve morale	400,000	2.00%	2.50%	3.00%	8,000	10,000	12,000
Motivated and efficient workforce	400,000	1.00%	1.50%	2.00%	4,000	6,000	8,000
Flexible staff	400,000	1.00%	1.50%	2.00%	4,000	6,000	8,000
					16,000	22,000	28,000
TOTAL SAVINGS					172,500	242,750	313,000

Appendix K: Graph of cost savings

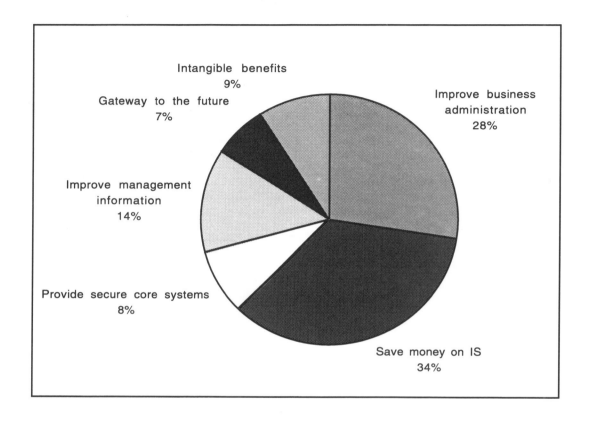

Appendix L: Assumptions for cost savings in organisation

Staff breakdown
Managerial	5
Stock	5
Purchasing	5
Finance	10
Sales administration	20
IS	5
	50

Staff costs

	No.	£	Cost per capita:
IS staff costs	5	100,000	20000
Managerial staff costs	5	250,000	50000
Other staff costs	40	400,000	10000
Total staff costs	50	750,000	

Information systems costs

IS maintenance costs	200,000
Specialist knowledge	100,000
IS staff costs	100,000
Total IS spend at present	400,000

Appendix M: Sample calculation of Net Present Value (NPV)

Bank base rate	6.0%
Additional charge	3.0%
Cost of capital =	9.0%

Assumptions :
(1)   Value of expected benefits last for four years.
(2)   The value of the benefits reduces by 30% each year on the previous year.

			1.000	0.917	0.842	0.772	0.708
					Expected Savings		
		Total	Year 0	Year 1	Year 2	Year 3	Year 4
Low							
	(Expenditure)/Savings		(283,474)	172,500	120,750	84,525	59,168
	NPV	83,601	(283,474)	158,257	101,633	65,269	41,916
Medium							
	(Expenditure)/Savings		(360,439)	242,750	169,925	118,948	83,263
	NPV	156,125	(360,439)	222,706	143,022	91,849	58,986
High							
	(Expenditure)/Savings		(485,651)	313,000	219,100	153,370	107,359
	NPV	180,402	(485,651)	287,156	184,412	118,430	76,056